# A.J. FOYT

# RACE CAR LEGENDS

## COLLECTOR'S EDITION

A.J. Foyt

The Allisons

Dale Earnhardt Jr.

Danica Patrick

Famous Finishes

Famous Tracks

The Jarretts

Jeff Burton

Jeff Gordon

Jimmie Johnson

Kenny Irwin Jr.

The Labonte Brothers

Lowriders

Mario Andretti

Mark Martin

Monster Trucks & Tractors

Motorcycles

The Need for Speed

Off-Road Racing

The Pit Crew

Rockcrawling

Rusty Wallace

Stunt Driving

Tony Stewart

The Unsers

# A.J. FOYT

Josh Wilker

**With additional text by**
**G.S. Prentzas**

An imprint of Infobase Publishing

**A.J. Foyt**
Copyright © 2007 by Infobase Publishing

Chelsea House
An imprint of Infobase Publishing
132 West 31st Street
New York NY 10001

ISBN-10: 0-7910-8759-X
ISBN-13: 978-0-7910-8759-6

**Library of Congress Cataloging-in-Publication Data**
Wilker, Josh.
  A.J. Foyt / Josh Wilker with additional text by G.S. Prentzas.
     p. cm. – (Race car legends. Collector's edition)
Includes bibliographical references and index.
ISBN 0-7910-8759-X
1. Foyt, A.J., 1935—Juvenile literature. 2. Automobile racing drivers–United States–Biography–Juvenile literature. I. Prentzas, G.S. II. Title. III. Series.
GV1032.F66W552 2007          796.72'092–dc22
[B]                                        2005020296

Series design by Erika K. Arroyo
Cover design by Hierophant Publishing Services/EON PreMedia/Joo Young An

Printed in the United States of America

Bang PH 10 9 8 7 6 5 4 3 2 1

This book is printed on acid-free paper.

# CONTENTS

# 1

# PLACES NO ONE ELSE WILL GO

All the other drivers stopped and stared as the kid walked by. They knew him. He was Tony Foyt's son. They'd seen him hanging around racetracks with his father, a mechanic, since he was a little boy. But they had never seen him like this. He was here to race.

Unlike the other drivers in their grease-stained T-shirts and jeans, Tony Foyt's son wore spotless white pants and a blazing red silk shirt. The pit area at Houston's Playland Park that night in 1953 buzzed with talk about the new driver in the gaudy outfit. Most rookies would have shied away from any extra attention. This lean, handsome 18-year-old, however, was not like other rookies.

As Anthony Joseph Foyt Jr. wheeled his midget race car onto the track, he knew the car was fast. At Tony Foyt's auto repair shop, father and son had worked together for many days to turn the car into a tough racing machine. Sometimes, if there was more work to be done, the younger Foyt labored all night long under the glare of the auto shop lights.

He knew the car well, but when he blasted around the dirt track during a **qualifying run**, he sensed something

18-year-old rookie A.J. Foyt drew a lot of attention at Playland Park in Houston, Texas, when he started racing in 1953.

was wrong. Ignoring wild cheers from the crowd, Foyt complained to his father that the car lacked power. Tony Foyt told his son to relax—he had just broken the Playland Park track record of Indianapolis 500 champion Johnnie Parsons. A.J.'s instincts were correct, though. Concerned that his excited son would try to go too fast in his new midget racer, Tony Foyt had secretly cut back the engine's power. The elder Foyt, who had been around racing all his life, had seen men crippled in flame-riddled crashes. He had seen men killed. A.J. knew the risks, too, having spent his whole life around racetracks.

Tony Foyt and his friend Jimmy Greer watched from the pit as A.J. took his place at the starting line for the first race of the night. The two men had scraped together every spare penny they had to build the car. They had scrambled to work every angle, finding a deal on a quality metal frame—a Kurtis Kraft chassis—and buying the high-powered Offenhauser engine from the widow of a driver who had died in a crash. They had gone without all luxuries. Greer and his family ate off a picnic table in a house with old sheets on the windows.

A.J. shot into the lead in the second **lap** of the four-lap dash and held on to win. He won the second race, too, sliding through the tricky turns of the quarter-mile oval like an old pro. By the beginning of the third race, fans crowding the fence at trackside were covered with dirt thrown from all the race cars' wheels. By the end of that race, they were muddier than ever and reeling with joyous disbelief. The kid had won again.

He took his place at the back of the pack to start the fourth and final race. Due to an inverted start—the fastest cars last and the slowest cars first—A.J. would have to pass every driver on the track to win. Many of the drivers had been manhandling race cars around the dirt track at Playland Park for years. They knew all the tricks and weren't afraid to use them.

A race on a dirt track at Playland Park in 1953, like other races on dirt tracks of the time, constantly teetered

Foyt tries to muscle his father's #2 midget car out of a jam during a race at Arrowhead Park, Houston, Texas.

on the brink of disaster. Winning was mostly a by-product of survival. Ruts and oil slicks laced a track surrounded only by a flimsy fence. The cockpits of the cars had no protective metal frames, and the drivers did not wear fire-proof suits. Drivers took a beating as they muscled their cars over the bumpy track. Rocks and stray shards of metal on the track flew up into the open cockpits.

Foyt later recalled, "In some ways, the early days are the most dangerous. You run races that aren't real fast, but you run 'em as hard as you can. The tracks aren't real good, the cars aren't real good, and a lot of the drivers aren't real good." Just to finish all four races on his first day in his new car would have been an accomplishment for a teenaged driver. But A.J. wanted more than that. The way he bulled the car through the turns, sending high rooster tails of dirt to the sky, set him apart from the other drivers.

The drivers gunned their engines, waiting for the race to start. In their rearview mirrors they all caught a glimpse of blazing red in the cockpit of the last car in the line. A.J., still wrapped in his regal silk shirt, fastened his helmet and slipped his goggles into place. Jimmy Greer leaned over and mouthed a common racing phrase. It is meant to encourage racers to throw fear out the window and pump the throttle with everything they've got. Jimmy Greer said to A.J., "Stand on it."

A.J. left four cars in the dust by the first turn. By the second turn, half the cars in the race were receding in his rearview mirror. He avoided two spinning cars by shooting low onto the grass and then hurtling back onto the track to continue his climb. He drove deeper and deeper into every corner, skidding within inches of the fence, grazing other cars as he slipped by. It didn't seem possible that he could be driving as he was and still be under control. Within a few laps he had passed all but one of the drivers.

A crafty veteran named Buddy Rackley guarded his lead. He ranged high and low to block the charging rookie. A.J. could not get past. Rackley hogged the inside in the second-to-last turn on the last lap and Foyt broke high. He edged forward through a sliver of daylight on the back straightaway, and the two cars sailed toward the final turn dead even. In the turn Rackley still held the inside. In an attempt to make the rookie back off, Rackley veered high, forcing Foyt toward the outer wall.

# MIDGET RACING

Midget racing became extremely popular in post–World War II America. Throughout the country, racing fans flocked to tracks to watch the small, fast cars fly around quarter-mile ovals. Many cars compete in midget races, which are usually hotly contested. The wheel-to-wheel action is often frenzied. The congested track often becomes a whirl of spins and crashes as the drivers steer their race cars toward the finish line. Many big-name drivers, including A.J. Foyt, started their careers on the midget circuits.

The race had whittled down to a single choice. Foyt could ease off the accelerator and settle for second-place money. Or he could attempt to gun it through a narrow opening and risk running his wheels over Rackley's—a sure way to catapult into a ferocious crash.

Automobile racers like Foyt know that taking risks can be thrilling. As biographer Bill Libby noted in his 1974 biography *Foyt*, two-time Indianapolis 500 champion Rodger Ward connected risk-taking with winning. He observed, "I will put myself in places on a racetrack that most drivers will not go." Ward would make this comment a decade after A.J. Foyt's debut at Playland Park. In the mid-1960s, the young charger from Texas would succeed Ward as United States Auto Club (**USAC**) national champion. Ward would also pay tribute to his successor by declaring, "Foyt is the greatest of drivers because he will put himself in places no one else will go."

As Rackley pushed him toward the wall, A.J. Foyt heard Jimmy Greer's voice in his head. The voice said, "Stand on it." A.J. stomped the throttle to the floor, and the **checkered flag** waved for him.

# 2

## "I GUESS YOU'RE GONNA BE A RACE DRIVER"

Anthony Joseph Foyt Jr. was born on January 16, 1935 in Houston, Texas. As a toddler, he followed his father to work. He soon came to love the gasoline-laced air of the B and F Garage. B and F stood for Burt and Foyt, partners in business and also a local racing team. Dale Burt drove, and Tony Foyt was the mechanic. A love of cars and racing ran in the Foyt family's blood. Tony's father had also been a mechanic. Tony himself had driven race cars, too. "I never won none of my races," he said. "We run for nothin'. We were more or less just having a bunch of fun." At the garage, Tony Foyt would place his son on a high metal stool in an attempt to keep him from getting in the way. But always, A.J. soon wriggled down from the high perch, eager to get closer to the action. He peppered his father with questions as the mechanic worked on an engine. His first questions about the world always seemed to concern the same subject. "That's all he had interest in—cars," Tony Foyt said.

## A VERY YOUNG START

A.J. started driving not too long after he learned how to walk. For his third birthday, he received a go-kart built by his father. A.J. spent hour after hour zooming around the outside of the house, imitating the drivers at the Houston racetracks. As the youngest member of the B and F racing team, A.J. got to see a lot of the professional drivers. And like those drivers, A.J. found he could pick up speed if he started his slide into the corners early.

When A.J. was five years old, his father built him his own midget racer. "I thought that little old car was the

A.J. Foyt appears to be a natural behind the wheel of his first car, a go-kart built by his father for his third birthday.

most beautiful thing there ever was," said A.J. Foyt about the blue and white car. His father remembered that A.J. would drive the midget as fast as it could go—about 50 miles an hour. A.J. got so good at flying around the yard in the midget that one night his dad set up a pre-race exhibition at the Houston Speed Bowl.

A.J. was only expected to take a lap around the track by himself, but he didn't see much point in that. So he

A precocious five-year-old Foyt challenged Doc Cossey to a race at the Houston Speed Bowl. The amazing youngster beat the veteran driver, even though Foyt's midget car had only three horsepower.

swaggered up to one of the best racers in Houston, a man named Doc Cossey, and said, "Doc, I can outrun that midget of yours." Cossey started chuckling and didn't stop until he was eating the dust of the five-year-old's quick start when the green flag dropped. A.J. whipped the car around the track like a seasoned veteran and won the race. "I guess it was then and there," he later reflected in his 1983 autobiography, *A.J.: The Life of America's Greatest Race Car Driver*, "I knew I wanted to be a race-car driver."

## RACING IN THE REAL THING

A.J. longed to get behind the wheel of the real thing, one of the two B and F midget racers. When he was 11 years old, his parents went to Dallas to race one of their cars. They left A.J. behind to babysit his little sister Marlene. He sensed that this was his big chance. With the help of three friends, he wheeled the racer that had been left behind out of the garage and managed to get it started. A.J. sent his friends into a whooping, hollering frenzy by blasting around the outside of his house at full throttle, lap after lap, faster each time. Then they were all shaken by a loud explosion, as the car's engine burst into flames.

Tony and Evelyn came home later that night. "The grass was chewed to pieces and there were tire gouges all around," Tony said. "The swings in the yard had been knocked down. I went into the house and right into his bedroom. He played like he was asleep, but he wasn't. I could tell."

A.J. was well aware that his father was a stern disciplinarian. He braced himself for the worst. From the other room came his mother's voice, "Don't say anything to him right now when you're so mad."

By the next morning, Tony Foyt had come to realize exactly what the incident meant. It wasn't that A.J. was out to disobey him. It was more that A.J. had something inside him, like a hunger. It needed feeding. When his son emerged from his room the next morning, Tony Foyt calmly said, "I guess you're gonna be a race driver, A.J."

By the time A.J. was halfway through his senior year of high school, he decided that he needed to chase his dream full time. "I couldn't study any more. I just couldn't wait any longer." He dropped out of school and started racing. His first races were in a 14-year-old **stock car**, a 1938 Ford that he had bought for $100. At the same time, he was sneaking his father's midget racer out to a local racetrack to run full-speed laps in the dark.

Foyt sits in the first race car he ever built — a 1938 Ford standard coupe.

At first, his father refused to consider making A.J. a part of his racing team. Instead, A.J. began by racing a banged-up midget car for a man named Red Fondren. The car was old and hard to control. "If a car doesn't handle," Foyt said about his first midget car, "you make it handle." By the time he was 18, A.J. started turning some heads with his ability to strong-arm a lesser car to the front of the pack.

## A FATHER'S FIX

Foyt deeply respected his father, Tony. As the young driver was gaining experience on racetracks throughout Texas and the Southwest, the elder Foyt often had to keep A.J.'s wildness in line. Once, during practice laps before a race, A.J. was goofing around, careening all over the track and getting very close to the guardrails. Tony told his son to stop it. A.J. ignored his father, but when he climbed out of the car, Tony tackled him. With the help of another man, Tony kept A.J. pinned to the ground until the race started. There was no better way to punish A.J. than not allowing him to race.

A.J. watches as his father, Tony Foyt Sr. tunes up his race car. A.J. had a close relationship with his father throughout his life.

One of those watching closely was his father, and he did not enjoy seeing his son careen dangerously around a dirt track in Fondren's rattling bucket of bolts. He told A.J., "You gotta get something better under you or quit."

"This thing has gone too far!" cried A.J.'s worried mother upon learning of Houston's newest racing partnership. "She didn't want me to drive race cars," said A.J. "But she stood behind me when I decided to do it. And she told me how good I was. She gave me some pride in what I was doing. She always encouraged me. 'You're as good as anybody else,' she said."

Foyt quickly started proving her right. After beating Buddy Rackley to sweep the card at Playland Park, Foyt ranged to tracks all over the Southwest to display an overpowering hunger for the checkered flag. Word spread fast among the other drivers: The kid in the silk shirt will beat you any way he can.

Plus, Foyt didn't mind backing up his brash racing tactics with his fists. His lifelong reputation as a hot-tempered brawler was born on the steamy dirt tracks of Texas, Oklahoma, and Louisiana. Everyone learned to stay clear of the volatile racing phenomenon, especially after a loss.

# 3

# "THIS KID CAN CUT IT"

To reach the Indianapolis 500 in the 1950s, drivers first had to prove themselves in the dangerous world of sprint car racing. A.J. Foyt started racing sprint cars in 1955, and he quickly realized why many drivers considered sprint car racing such a challenge. Foyt said, "They're the most powerful cars you can run on short tracks. . . . Sprint cars race on dirt tracks and I was always good on dirt tracks. Racing dirt, on a short track, it's more driver than car, and I like that."

Foyt soon showed that he could handle a sprint car. In 1957, Wally Meskowski asked the young driver to join his prominent racing team. Foyt ran more than 50 races that year, nearly a race per week. He ran them all with reckless abandon. Foyt wanted to get to the top, and he didn't care too much about the risks.

Reigning USAC champion Jimmy Bryan noticed Foyt. Bryan, a hard-charging driver himself, recommended Foyt to his boss, IndyCar owner Al Dean. It didn't take long for Dean to size up the young driver. Early in 1958 Dean declared, "This kid can cut it." With that, Foyt finally had his ride for the Indianapolis 500.

## SPRINT CARS

Sprint car racing is one of the oldest types of motor sports in the United States. The small cars have powerful engines and are easy to maneuver. The races are usually run on dirt tracks, which get bumpy after the racers have completed a few laps. The lightweight cars easily go airborne when they hit a rut. Sprint car racing is very dangerous, and many drivers have been killed in races.

A.J. Foyt, in the #1 car, won this race against Gary Bettenhausen (#11) at the 1968 Hoosier Hundred, held at the Indiana State Fairgrounds, in Indianapolis, Indiana.

## GETTING INITIATED TO INDY

When Foyt began preparing for the race, the speedway overwhelmed him. The sheer size of the place awed him. The grandstands could hold more than a quarter of a million people. The track itself was five times bigger than any track he had ever raced on. The imposing history of the place also intimidated him. Some of the greatest triumphs in racing had occurred at the speedway, and some of the greatest racers had built their reputations there. He wondered whether he could take his place among them. Briefly, he questioned whether he belonged at the track at all.

Any doubts faded as soon as Foyt got behind the wheel. A veteran named Pat O'Connor gave the rookie some basic

Mechanic Clint Brawner *(standing, left)* shares the wheel with A.J. Foyt. IndyCar owner Al Dean *(far right)* is seated beside Foyt.

tips and then led Foyt around the track for a few laps. Foyt soon found his own best path around the track—what the racers call "the groove." He qualified for twelfth position, the highest of any rookie driver that year.

In his first Indy 500, Foyt was close enough to the front to witness a deadly crash in the first lap that involved nearly half of the 33 cars in the race. The two front-runners, Ed Elisian and Dick Rathmann, tangled in turn three, causing the third-place driver, Jimmy Reece, to slow. Bob Veith hit Reece. Then O'Connor's car hit Reece's, flew 50 feet into the air, and exploded into flames upon impact with the ground. The chain reaction continued as Jerry Unser's

Pat O'Connor helped Foyt before his first Indianapolis 500, but then a crash claimed O'Connor's life in the first lap.

car flipped up and over a wall and more than a dozen cars reeled and spun. Foyt muscled his car into a slide to slow it down and slipped through a narrow opening between two cars to escape the crash unharmed.

The **yellow flag** slowed the race to a crawl for 20 laps as track workers cleared the wreckage. Foyt stole a glance at O'Connor's flame-blackened car and knew instantly that the man who had showed him around the track was dead. For the rest of the race, Foyt drove as if enveloped in fog. "The spirit wasn't there," said Foyt. For the first time in his life, he drove tentatively. His race ended on lap 148, when his car skidded in water from a broken hose and then traveled a thousand feet backward before hitting a wall.

Foyt vowed that he would be back, but tougher and harder the next time. There would be only one thing on his mind: winning. "I would never get close to any race driver again," Foyt said.

In the 1959 Indy 500, Foyt charged from his starting position in the middle of the pack to get as close as fifth by the time the race was half over. After a minor collision with another car however, his car slowed down. He came in tenth. "Close isn't enough," Foyt grumbled after the race. "You win or you lose. I can win, but I don't think the car can."

Foyt's dissatisfaction with the Dean racing team—and with its mechanic, Clint Brawner—grew as the year went on. Foyt won three USAC races, but he was sure he could have won more. At the end of the season, he broke with Dean to race for Bob Bowes. The Bowes team mechanic, George Bignotti, was building a reputation not unlike Foyt's own. He was known for doing anything to win.

Foyt's relationship with Bignotti was stormy from the start. The two very competitive men bickered constantly. After another disappointing finish at Indy in 1960, Foyt declared to his wife, Lucy, whom he had married five years earlier, "I'm no better off than I was with Clint Brawner." Foyt threatened to quit racing. Lucy convinced him to try one more race. It was sound advice.

Foyt started to win. He almost pushed Bignotti to the breaking point, but the team was nearly impossible to beat. Going into a late season race in Phoenix, Arizona, Foyt only needed to finish in the middle of the pack to snare the USAC crown away from the reigning champion, Rodger Ward.

As the 1961 season began, the streaking racer again set his sights on the Indianapolis 500. In the qualifying

A.J. Foyt *(left)* stands next to his wife, Lucy, and his parents, Evelyn and Tony.

rounds, a flamboyant driver named Eddie Sachs snagged **pole position** for the country's biggest race. Sachs, known as The Clown Prince of Racing, loved to put on a show for the fans at Indy. One year, he brought in his own jazz band to play concerts from the infield. Another year, the spirit moved him to jump into the prerace parade to wave at the crowd with an imaginary baton.

Foyt started the race from the seventh position. He had not made as much noise about winning as the boastful Sachs in the days leading up to the race. But that didn't mean he wasn't supremely confident. On the day of the race, Foyt motioned to the pace car that was always given to the winner of the 500 and vowed to his mother that he would win the car.

# 4

## A TOUGH CHAMPION

The 1961 Indianapolis 500 featured spectacular racing from the start. Jim Hurtubise blasted out in front in the first lap. The young driver, who had earlier followed up a blazing qualifying run by proclaiming that the hallowed Brickyard "ain't so tough," took the lead for 35 laps.

When Hurtubise's engine went sour, Rufus Parnell Jones (better known as Parnelli Jones) took over. Then a chunk of loose debris from an earlier wreck kicked up and struck Jones in the forehead. He kept his car in front as blood gushed down into his goggles. Jones led the pack for 75 miles but eventually dropped back with mechanical troubles. Eddie Sachs then claimed the lead, but Foyt was close behind. Sachs knew how to handle a car, so Foyt knew he had his work cut out for him.

Foyt gambled and stayed on the inside track on a turn, almost catching the grassy infield that would have sent him spinning. He managed to squeeze past Sachs, but Sachs jumped back in front in the straightaway. "There was no question that his car was faster than mine," Foyt said, "so I knew I would have to outdrive him in the corners."

Time and again, Foyt found narrow openings through which to sneak past Sachs in the corners, only to see his lead turn to dust in the straightaways. The two men traded first place 10 times as the race wore on. Lucy Foyt spoke for the electrified crowd when she later recalled, "It was like it was hard to breathe."

The two drivers locked in the duel both began to wonder whether they and their cars could hold up under the strain. "There was no margin for error, no room for mistake," Sachs said. "It was a matter of which one of us would break first." Foyt, for his part, had the utmost faith in Bignotti's ability to build a car that would last the entire race. He was not immune to the pressure, however, admitting, "Your nerves cause you to sort of hallucinate at times."

With 30 miles to go, both men made pit stops for what they hoped would be the final time. Coming back out onto the track, Foyt could sense something different about his car. As if it had somehow shucked off weight, the car felt faster. He blasted by Sachs and started building a lead. Foyt could almost taste the victory when a pit member flashed him a sign that read, "Fuel low." A fuel line had clogged on the last pit stop. The lighter fuel tank had given Foyt extra speed, but it also would apparently cost him the race. He had to pull into the pit again as Sachs sped on toward an apparent win.

There seemed to be no way now for Foyt to triumph, but still he pushed on, desperately, not allowing Sachs to ease up. His dogged pursuit paid off. With only five laps left, the white warning layer appeared on Sachs's right rear tire, telling him that his tire was wearing out. "At the speeds Eddie was running trying to stay ahead," said Foyt, "he had

Foyt's Bowes crew finishes up a quick pit stop for tires and fuel during the 1961 Indianapolis 500.

worn through the tread rubber." Sachs could either drive into the pit area for new tires and lose the race, or hope that the tire held up. If it held, he would win. If it didn't, he would crash. It was the type of decision Foyt himself had been faced with many times, going back to his battle with Buddy Rackley in Houston. Foyt always risked the worst for a chance at winning.

But not Sachs. He headed for a visit with his pit crew. "I'd rather finish second than finish dead," he said later. Foyt accelerated into the lead, this time for

Foyt pulls away from Eddie Sachs and goes on to take the checkered flag in the first of his four Indianapolis 500 victories. The 26-year-old Foyt beat Sachs by 8.28 seconds.

good. Nearly any driver in Sachs's position would have done as Sachs did. Foyt was different. After winning his first Indianapolis 500, he gave credit to Sachs but confided that if their roles had been reversed, "I'd have gone on."

## PUSHING FOR PERFECTION

Foyt took the checkered flag at 18 other USAC races that year to win his second straight national championship. He became the youngest driver ever to win both Indy and the national championship in the same year. Still, such an honor wasn't enough to make him take a break. No one worked harder than Foyt. Longtime racing team crew chief Ray Nichels said of him, "He'll try anything and he'll go from sunup to sundown to get the job done. If it's not finished then, he'll work around the clock." Foyt's constant striving for perfection eventually put him at odds with his mechanic. Bignotti wearied of Foyt's constant second-guessing his mechanical decisions. "A.J. is not the easiest guy to get along with," he said. Years later, Foyt was able to admit that "our biggest problem was that George was an absolute genius on engines and I knew enough to bother him."

The feud between the two reached a breaking point at the 1962 Indianapolis 500. First, failing brakes caused Foyt to fall out of the lead. Then, a few laps later, Foyt's left rear wheel flew off, ending his race. The mechanical failures made the toppled champion rage. "The only man in the crew I can trust is my father," Foyt fumed. Bignotti and Foyt parted ways soon after.

Neither man was able to find much success for the rest of the year. Rodger Ward used his second Indy 500 win as a springboard to the 1962 USAC national championship. Ward found fault with his rival's hard-charging style by saying, "He runs too hard, too often, and takes too much out of his equipment." And Ward wasn't the only one taking aim at Foyt. "Everyone wants to beat Foyt. It gives the boys a big laugh," Foyt noted bitterly. He realized that the only way he would be able to turn back all his challengers would be to reunite with Bignotti.

Foyt completed all 12 of the IndyCar races he entered in 1963. His finishes earned him enough points to reclaim the USAC championship. And after cruising to victory in two sports-car road races in Nassau, the Bahamas, Foyt began to make his mark as a driver who could win in any kind of car and on any kind of track.

## LEGENDARY INDY 500 CHAMPIONS

Since its start in 1911, the Indianapolis 500 has attracted many of the world's best drivers. Winners include such legends as Louie Meyer (1928, 1933, 1936); Wilbur Shaw (1937, 1939, 1940); Mauri Rose (1941, 1947, 1948); Bill Vukovich (1953, 1954); Bobby Unser (1968, 1975, 1981); Mario Andretti (1969); Al Unser (1970, 1971, 1978); Gordon Johncock (1973, 1982); Johnny Rutherford (1974, 1976, 1980); Rick Mears (1979, 1984, 1991); and Emerson Fittipaldi (1989, 1993). Recent champions include Helio Castroneves (2001, 2002); Dan Wheldon (2005); and Sam Hornish, Jr. (2006). A.J. Foyt is the only four-time winner, having taken the check- ered flag in 1961, 1964, 1967, and 1977.

## FOYT CHALLENGES NEW TECHNOLOGY

Foyt also spent time in 1963 testing tires for Goodyear at the Indianapolis Speedway. Foyt's keen feel for a race car helped Goodyear develop tires that eventually out- performed those of longtime Indy 500 tire maker Fire- stone. Foyt's long hours of testing at the speedway did more than just help Goodyear tires. "The thousands of miles I put in at Indy didn't hurt me, either," he said. "I know this ol' track pretty good now. It's very tricky and it takes time to get to know it. I know every bump in the road. . . . I know the way the wind blows different places. You can only get that running here, and not just in races."

In 1964, it seemed at first that Foyt's intimate knowl- edge of the speedway would not be enough to give him a win. In the month leading up to the race, all the talk among race fans was about the revolutionary rear-engine cars.

Two years earlier, some European drivers and an American racer named Dan Gurney had started to bring them onto the track. At first they couldn't compete with the conventional front-engine cars. By 1964, however, it was clear that the rear-engine cars were faster.

A skeptical A.J. Foyt sounded an alarm about the rear-engine cars to anyone who would listen. "These new cars just seem like a bunch of sticks strung together with chicken wire," he said. "Instead of tucking the tanks away from you, there are fuel tanks all around the cockpit and they're full of gasoline, which is a lot more explosive than alcohol. They surround you with stuff that can blow you to kingdom come in a second."

Most of the top racers chose to ignore Foyt's warning. Sachs, growing desperate for a win at Indy, spoke for many drivers when he said, "We'll lose to 'em if we don't take our chances with 'em." Foyt was never against taking a chance if

Rookie driver Dave MacDonald is pictured in his ill-fated rear-engine car prior to the 1964 Indianapolis 500.

it meant getting a shot at victory. But he figured that he had that shot already. As Bignotti said, referring to the European racers, "The Grand Prix guys simply know more about these cars than we do. But we know more about this race than they do." Foyt figured that to take a chance in a dangerous new car would be to take too dangerous a gamble.

In the second lap of the 1964 Indy 500, a rookie driver named Dave MacDonald lost control of his rear-engine car. MacDonald hit a bump in the track in the fourth turn. He smacked the inner wall and then—his car aflame and spinning wildly—crashed against the outer wall. Sachs, who had been trailing MacDonald tightly, was helpless. His car speared MacDonald's and then exploded on impact with the wall. Foyt came out of the second turn on the opposite side of the track to see cars spinning and sliding in every direction and twin columns of thick black smoke rising from the cars of Sachs and MacDonald. "It looked like an atomic bomb had dropped," Foyt later said.

The Indianapolis 500 came to a stop. The race had been halted only once before in the entire history of the speedway, and that time had been for rain. In the 105 minutes it took for workers to clean up the track, Foyt did not allow himself to think about what nearly everyone at the speedway knew. Sachs had died immediately, and MacDonald would die a few hours later in a hospital bed. Foyt said, "I didn't want to know. There would be time for me to know later." He knew that he had to put the crash out of his mind to focus on the race.

Soon afterward, the race resumed, and Foyt took over. His relentlessly competitive spirit steeled him against the haunting image of the crash. He methodically built a lead that no one could beat. As other racers allowed thoughts

A burning tire flies toward spectators during the gasoline explosion that resulted from a crash during the 1964 Indianapolis 500. Drivers Dave MacDonald and Eddie Sachs lost their lives in the accident.

of the crash to slip into their minds, Foyt pressed on. Even the great Rodger Ward admitted, "I made mistakes. I was shaken by what happened. I was seeing ghosts, I guess." Ward, in second, dropped farther and farther behind. Foyt pressed on, hungry for speed and victory. He lapped the entire field, winning in record time.

In a somber Victory Lane, Foyt finally let the bad news sink in. He couldn't speak for a few moments. Then he managed to say, "I'm sorry. I'm sorry those guys died.

Foyt acknowledges his fans in Victory Lane after winning the 1964 Indianapolis 500.

They were my friends." Foyt paid tribute to MacDonald and said that Sachs "had more guts than any of us."

Soot and grime covered Foyt's face; his lips were raw and cracked. His rumpled, dirty racing suit had been blown wide open at the elbow during the race. "You got to carry on," he said. "You can't let anyone get too close to you in this game. If they get killed, it breaks your heart. And if you're going to race, you've got to race alone."

# 5

**"I WENT FLYING"**

After the tragedy at the 1964 Indy 500, Foyt went on to capture his first win at a race of the National Association for Stock Car Auto Racing (**NASCAR**) on July 4 in Daytona. There, he captured the checkered flag beating out stock car great Bobby Isaac in the last lap.

At an IndyCar race at Langhorne, Pennsylvania, the track temperature soared to 132 degrees, and some of the steering controls in Foyt's car failed. But it was not the end for Foyt—he just cranked a little harder on the steering wheel and won anyway. In Trenton, New Jersey, the track temperature reached 140 degrees. Rodger Ward led the race before collapsing in the pits. Jim McElreath took over until he, too, wilted in the heat. "Was it hot out there?" asked an unstoppable Foyt in Victory Lane. "I'll have to ask some of the boys about that."

Foyt set a record for most consecutive Indycar wins— seven—by holding off Bobby Marshman at Springfield, Illinois, by less than a second. His ninth win, at the Indianapolis Fairgrounds, set the record for most Indycar wins in a season and gave him 25 Indycar victories in his career, another record. He celebrated by roaring past Parnelli Jones at Sacramento for career win number 26.

A.J. Foyt and his pit crew chief, George Bignotti, receive awards from Irvin Fried, owner of the Langhorne Speedway. Foyt virtually clinched his fourth USAC national championship in June 1964 by winning the 100-mile race in Langhorne, Pennsylvania.

## A TERRIBLE CRASH

Win number 27 was a little harder to come by. In January 1965, on his way to a stock car race in Riverside, California, Foyt was struck by a gloomy premonition. "I called Lucy from the airport and told her exactly where I had parked the car and reminded her where the extra key was hidden," he recalled. "I had never done that before."

During the race, Foyt's brakes failed just as he was making a move in the second turn of the Riverside track to blast past Junior Johnson and Marvin Panch. Foyt had a choice: Plow Panch into the upper wall and stay on the track, or jerk the car off the course and pray. "If you've gotta go," said Foyt, "you do your damnedest not to take anyone with you."

One of Foyt's front wheels caught in a hole in the dirt as he careened off the track. He shot off a 35-foot wall and flew 50 feet, cartwheeling end over end and finally crashing bottom-side up. Parnelli Jones rushed to the wreckage and cleared dirt from his suffocating rival's mouth. Foyt wasn't dead, but he was banged up worse than he ever had been before. He had a bad concussion, a broken back, a crushed sternum, a broken left heel, cuts and torn flesh on his face and hands, and, as he said later, "My whole body was a mass of bruises." He regained consciousness a day after the crash to phone his mother to tell her he was all right and then passed out again for another day.

Foyt refused to accept his doctor's opinion that he would never be able to race again. By swimming daily and taking long walks, Foyt was ready to get back to racing after only three months. At the track in Phoenix, Foyt had to use a cane to get around. Constant jolts of pain shot up his back. Instead of screaming in agony, which is what he later admitted he wanted to do, Foyt joked with the other racers about the terrible crash and then went out and won the pole position.

At a stock car race a week later in Atlanta, the pain in Foyt's back was so intense that it was causing his vision to blur. He kept the car in the race until the throttle—the valve that controls the amount of fuel that flows into the engine—stuck in the wide-open position. Foyt could not slow down and, as he put it, "I went flying high, wide, and handsome." He escaped this crash unscathed. In fact, when teammate Marvin Panch collapsed from heat exhaustion, Foyt took over and drove Panch's car to victory.

Foyt labored through mishap after mishap in 1965. "Maybe it's time to quit," he mused, after the gearbox in his racer gave way in mile 300 of the Indy 500. "Everything has gone wrong for me this year." But no matter how wrong things went, and no matter what he said to the contrary, Foyt refused to quit.

## TIME FOR CHANGES

Foyt began to look for reasons for his string of bad luck. George Bignotti could sense that he would be blamed. After his engine overheated at a 1965 race in Langhorne, Pennsylvania, Foyt announced, "I was going to give up racing, but I decided to give up my mechanic instead." Bignotti seemed almost relieved that his tumultuous union with Foyt had finally been severed. "He's not an easy man to beat," Bignotti said, "but maybe it'll be easier to beat him than live with him."

It seemed that no one could keep pace with Foyt. As he tried to regain the form that had brought him to the top, he worked harder than ever. Foyt tried everything, but the bad luck continued. He watched as Europeans Jimmy Clark and Graham Hill took the Indy 500 in 1965 and 1966, respectively. He watched as a young man named Mario Andretti captured the USAC championship in both 1965 and 1966. There were some who thought that Foyt simply was trying to do too much on his own; that he should focus only on driving and leave management and mechanical responsibilities to his support team.

## A MASTER MECHANIC

George Bignotti grew up in California, where his two older brothers raced cars. Although he sometimes jumped into the cockpit as a substitute driver, George was more of a whiz in the garage and focused on getting his brothers' cars ready for races. In 1954, he got his shot at the big leagues. He was hired to prepare a car for that year's Indianapolis 500. When the car finished sixth, Bignotti suddenly became a sought-after mechanic on the circuit. During his long career, Bignotti teamed up with such first-rate drivers as A.J. Foyt, Mario Andretti, Gordon Johncock, Tom Sneva, and Al Unser. With Bignotti holding the wrench, Foyt won the Indianapolis 500 twice (1961 and 1964) and the USAC championship three times. Bignotti was inducted into the International Motorsports Hall of Fame in 1993.

A.J. Foyt *(right)* and mechanic George Bignotti had a tumultuous relationship, but Bignotti was by Foyt's side for many of his victories.

Jim Clark, in the #82 car, takes the lead during the 1965 Indianapolis 500. Clark is followed by Foyt (#1) and Parnelli Jones (#98). Although Foyt worked hard throughout 1965 and 1966, he faced one disappointment after another.

In Milwaukee, in 1966, Foyt was dealt his biggest dose of hard luck yet. He slammed into a wall during a practice run, after part of his car broke. The collision ruptured a gas tank, and the car burst into flames. The flames scorched Foyt's hands, leaving severe burns. For weeks he was unable even to go to the bathroom without the help of his wife. His record string of 82 straight races on the USAC championship trail ended. More significantly, he had time to consider his career and racing. As Foyt put it, "Suddenly I had all kinds of time to think about a lot of things I hadn't thought about before." All the close calls he had been in on the racetrack came back to him. As Foyt wrote in his autobiography years later, "I realized there are some things I fear."

Foyt explains how he escaped death by leaping from his car after it hit a retaining wall and exploded. Foyt suffered burns on his face and hands in the crash, which occurred on a Milwaukee racetrack in June 1966.

Doubts lingered when he finally got back to racing. He managed to push them to the back of his mind by driving, as he said, "harder than I really wanted to. . . . By pushing myself harder than I did before, I did start winning again, and that's the greatest therapy in the world."

A.J. Foyt hired Tony Foyt Sr. *(right)* as his head mechanic, and together they built their own car for the Indy 500.

At the beginning of the 1967 racing season, Foyt hired a new head mechanic: Tony Foyt. The younger Foyt realized that he had been trying to do too much. "My dad has joined our racing team and taken a lot of decision-making and detail work off my shoulders," Foyt announced to reporters. As they had years before with that first midget racer, father and son worked together to build their own car for the 1967 Indy 500. The bright red Coyote, as A.J. Foyt called the design, could fly. For the first time in three years, A.J. Foyt felt confident about the race.

# 6

## "IT'S MY TIME NOW"

At the 1967 Indianapolis 500, A.J. Foyt would have to beat a revolutionary **turbo** car piloted by Parnelli Jones. Though it ran smoother and weighed half as much as other racing engines, the state-of-the-art engine in this car produced enough power to blast Jones around the track at record speeds. Most of the drivers that year were intimidated by Jones's new car, but Foyt wasn't among them. He brashly predicted, "It won't last half the race. Sooner or later the engine will overheat or the gearbox will go and it will be gone. It may be the car of the future . . . [b]ut no new car comes here and sorts itself out right away. Its time may come, but it's my time now."

On race day, Jones's car glided out to an early lead. When heavy rain halted the action after only 18 laps, Jones was leading his closest pursuer by a wide lead of 12 seconds. Foyt's confidence still held. Officials decided to resume the race the following day. "I'm so sure I'm gonna win this race," Foyt told Indianapolis Speedway owner Tony Hulman, "I ought to charge you for keeping my money overnight."

All eyes were on Parnelli Jones when he raced this state-of-the-art turbo car in the 1967 Indianapolis 500, but the car failed with only three laps to go. Foyt continued on to take the checkered flag.

That night, Foyt dreamed that he led the race. Then, in the last lap, with the race all but won, he turned a corner into a fiery pileup. Cars spun all over the track, and he had no place to go but straight into the crash. The nightmare shook Foyt awake.

When the leap race restarted, Jones managed to double his 12-second lead by the 50-lap mark. The high, whining sound of his car's engine seemed to mock all the roaring, laboring, engines in the other cars. The Indianapolis 500 began to resemble a bunch of pack mules in futile pursuit of a racehorse. "I had been certain he was going to break," said Foyt of Jones in the turbo car. "But when he got past the midway mark and kept going, I figured I was finished. All I could do was keep as much pressure on him as possible and hope for the best. But about the best I could do at that point was stay in the same lap with him."

While Jones's turbo car held everyone's attention, Foyt was running a brilliant race. Jones's lead was big, but the gap between Foyt and the car behind him was twice as big. There were 50 miles to go. Foyt kept the pressure on Parnelli by "driving harder than I had ever driven." Finally, with just three laps to go, the turbo car crumbled under the strain. Jones steered his powerless car into the pit and Foyt took over.

With the race all but won, Foyt sped through the last turn. Then, without quite understanding why, he slowed his car to a crawl. "It was as though I had a premonition," he said. "I dreamed about it, and then I came around the

A.J. Foyt threads his way through the wreckage of four cars on the last lap of the 1967 Indianapolis 500. It was a scene eerily like a dream he had the night before.

corner and there it was." The nightmare crash had come true. Cars were spinning and crashing into the track walls. "If I hadn't already slowed down," said Foyt, "there was no way I could have gotten through it." Foyt tried to sneak through on the inside but quickly saw that there was no hole. He cranked his car to the outside, calmly pumping his brakes, and squeezed past the disaster to a short stretch of open road and what he called "that bee-you-tea-ful checker waving at me."

## TAKING A SHOT AT LE MANS

It was important to Foyt to show the world that he could excel in every type of race there was. For that reason, just one week after his triumph at the Indianapolis 500, he set out for France to compete at Le Mans, the biggest sports car race in the world. It was a race that no American had ever won before.

The race, a 24-hour marathon, teamed Foyt with Dan Gurney, a sports car specialist. Foyt quickly got the hang of the road course, and during the race he actually turned in faster lap times than his more experienced partner. Foyt could not be defeated. The Americans broke the course record with a wider lead on the second place finisher than any winner had ever driven before.

After making Europe's most prestigious race look like a vacationer's Sunday drive, Foyt came home to go after the USAC national championship. Foyt's head-to-head battle with two-time defending national champion Mario Andretti came down to the last race of the season, in Phoenix, Arizona. Holding a slight edge in the overall standings, Foyt needed only to finish near the top of the race to secure the championship. Andretti was leading the

Drivers rush to their cars at the start of the 24-hour endurance race held in Le Mans, France. Foyt and codriver Dan Gurney won the 1967 competition in a Ford MK IV.

race and appeared a lock to take his third straight championship when Foyt was involved in a crash with another car. Always having all the angles covered, however, Foyt had worked out a deal with driver Roger McCluskey before the race. When Foyt crashed, McCluskey zoomed into the pit and jumped from his car so that Foyt could jump in, finish the race, and clinch the USAC crown. Andretti observed, "Foyt will do anything to win."

## SETTING HIS SIGHTS ON STOCK CARS

In 1972, Foyt made some noise on the stock car circuit. The biggest race held by NASCAR was the Daytona 500. Foyt had served notice back in 1971 that he was setting

A.J. Foyt, in the #21 stock car, Buddy Baker (#71), and Richard Petty (#43) race three abreast at the Texas World Speedway, College Station, Texas, in November 1972.

his sights on that race's checkered flag when he won pole position and battled Buddy Baker and Richard Petty for the lead for much of the race. A fuel problem kept him from winning that year, but he came back in 1972 with a vengeance.

The 1972 Daytona 500 turned into a two-man race not long after the green flag came down. Foyt and NASCAR legend Petty dueled, wheel to wheel, at 160 miles per hour. Petty had already won the race three times in the past. He would go on to win the Daytona 500 a record seven times and would win more than 200 NASCAR races in all.

## NASCAR BASICS

The National Association for Stock Car Auto Racing (NASCAR) was organized in 1947. At that time, the drivers drove actual stock cars—the kind of car that anyone could buy from a dealership's stock. NASCAR starting allowing modifications, however, and the races moved from bumpy dirt tracks to paved ovals. Today, NASCAR race cars have little in common with real dealership stock cars. Legendary racing families—such as the Pettys, Pearsons, Jarretts, Earnhardts, and Allisons—helped popularize NASCAR.

The two living legends electrified the crowd for the first half of the 1972 race, swapping the lead 12 times in 200 miles. Foyt then started to pull away from his rival. Petty's car cracked just trying to keep up. He watched from the pits, his useless, smoking car nearby, as Foyt lapped the field. The triumphant Foyt had set a track record that would stand for eight years. After this race he exclaimed, "I especially like to beat the best in the big ones. When you beat Petty and the rest of the NASCAR racers, you know you're beating the best."

On Foyt's home turf, however, a feeling of disappointment mounted. Back at Indianapolis, it suddenly seemed to Foyt that everything that could go wrong would go wrong. In 1975, a desperate qualifying run gave Foyt pole position for the second straight year. He led the race for 47 laps before falling behind. Then, late in the race, when he was within striking distance of the leaders, debris from a crash damaged his tires. A lengthy pit stop to remedy the problem dashed his hopes, and Foyt finished third. The following year, he came in second to

NASCAR champion Richard Petty *(left)* shakes hands with A.J. Foyt at the Indianapolis Motor Speedway. Petty and Foyt were fierce competitors, thrilling crowds on the stock car circuit.

Johnny Rutherford, who had gained the lead by cleverly running full throttle for 23 seconds under the yellow caution flag and won the race when it was stopped due to rain after only 102 laps.

# 7

## THE FINAL LAPS

After two near misses, Foyt wanted his fourth Indy 500 win more than ever. But the 42-year-old driver decided to approach the 1977 race differently than he ever had before—calmly. Foyt's new serene, even-handed approach was put to the test during the practice runs for the race. During those runs, old rival Mario Andretti edged Foyt in a much-hyped contest to become the first driver to circle the speedway track while averaging 200 miles per hour. Foyt stomached that defeat and also shrugged off a loss to Tom Sneva in the struggle for pole position. Foyt had bigger victories in his sights. This, Foyt said, was "one of those races when I felt I was going to win from the start. . . . I felt it with my steak and eggs that morning and I felt it as my challengers fell off, one by one."

With fewer than a hundred miles to go in the race, Foyt had only one man left to beat. Trailing by nearly 40 seconds, Foyt started to make his move on Gordon Johncock, the defending USAC national champion. He jumped to within striking distance by charging full throttle for a few seconds under the yellow caution flag. Using the same trick that Johnny Rutherford had used to beat him in 1976 was not below Foyt. He would do almost anything to win.

Foyt, driving his #14 Coyote, had to get by reigning USAC national champion Gordon Johncock (#20) to win the 1977 Indianapolis 500.

At 190 miles per hour, Foyt started turning in the fastest laps of the race. Johncock saw his lead shrink to a mere four seconds. Foyt's blood-red number 14 Coyote soon passed Johncock's car. Johncock's mechanic was Foyt's old mechanic and sparring partner George Bignotti. With 15 laps remaining, Johncock's car crawled to a halt when a valve spring broke. Foyt roared on to become the first man in the 66-year history of the Indy 500 to win the race four times.

People started to wonder when Foyt would announce his retirement, but he was far from ready. In 1979, for a record seventh time, he won the USAC national championship. It seemed as if nothing could slow the aging racer down.

## A DEATH BRINGS PERSONAL CHANGES

In 1983, though, there finally came a day when Foyt did not want to race. He sat at the bedside of his sick father in a hospital room in Houston. Tony Foyt, who had been diagnosed with cancer, brought up the subject of a 24-hour sports car race being held at Daytona. Tony told his son to go run the race. The marathon race became a labor of love for the younger Foyt. He had never driven a Porsche before, and he hadn't driven in a sports car race since his 1967 win at Le Mans. But he grabbed the wheel of the unfamiliar car and, driving his heart out through fog and pouring rain, turned in faster lap times than anyone else in the race.

After leading his team to victory, Foyt let his two French teammates split the prize money while he took the trophy back to his father in Houston. Tony Foyt died a few months later, after watching Foyt qualify for the Indy 500 for a record twenty-sixth straight time. Foyt's mother Evelyn had died two years earlier, also just after getting to see Foyt qualify.

Foyt struggled after his father's death. He had lost not only his father, but also his mentor, his best friend, and his team manager. Friends and crew began to notice that Foyt had become mellower. When a wheel flew off of his car during a race at Phoenix, crew members braced themselves for one of Foyt's legendary tantrums. Instead, the mellowing racer simply handed out some constructive criticism. The burning desire to win at all costs had diminished. Foyt also began to spend more time with his family.

In 1985, the graying competitor entered America's oldest professional sports car race, the 12 Hours of Sebring. The grueling race served as an additional confirmation of Foyt's

## 12 HOURS OF SEBRING

Built atop a former Air Force base in Florida, the Sebring International Raceway hosted the first 12 Hours of Sebring in March 1952. Modeled after France's legendary 24 Hours of Le Mans race, Sebring features cars of different types competing at the same time in a thrilling road race. Custom-built racers compete in two Prototype classes (P1 and P2), and modified sports cars compete in two Grand Touring classes (GT1 and GT2). Winners have included such racing legends at Stirling Moss, Juan Fangio, Phil Hill, and Mario Andretti. In 1985, A.J. Foyt won the 12 Hours of Sebring. It was the last win of his career.

Bob Wolleck (*left*) celebrates with codriver A.J. Foyt after winning the 12 Hours of Sebring in 1985. They averaged 113.787 miles per hour over 281 laps.

growing status as a living legend. Only 31 out of the 78 cars that started the race were able to finish. Waiting until the end of the marathon to push his car to the limit, Foyt fended off a late charge by sports car champion Derek Bell and won.

By the end of the 1980s, Foyt found himself competing against the children of old rivals—drivers such as Mario Andretti's son, Michael, and Al Unser's son, Al. Racing's elder statesman began to reflect on the changing nature of his sport. Racing teams could no longer build a car by themselves. They now needed experts in various fields, such as aerodynamics, to help them build a competitive car. The days when one man could simply will himself to victory were over. Still, Foyt remained in the thick of the action, a living reminder of a tougher era of racing.

## THE END OF THE ROAD

Foyt broke both his legs in a crash at Elkhart Lake, Illinois, in 1990. After a difficult recovery and rehabilitation, he returned to racing in 1992. Foyt dazzled the fans at Indy by qualifying for the front row along with fellow racing legends Rick Mears and Mario Andretti. Foyt made the race in 1993, too. But that year a stunned Indianapolis Motor Speedway crowd, gathered for the first day of qualifying, listened as Foyt proclaimed what was once unthinkable. He told the crowd that a practice lap crash involving the driver of one of his cars had convinced him that he needed to spend more time managing his racing team. Not quite able to hold back the sobs, he told the crowd that his days as a racer were over.

A year later, in August 1994, the speedway entered a new era by holding its first stock car race, the Brickyard 400. Sports car racers, short track specialists, IndyCar champions, and all of the top NASCAR drivers flocked to what would be the most well-attended stock car race with the most prize money ever. Even after announcing his retirement as a racer, Foyt could not resist. He was among more than 80 racers fighting for 43 spots in the race. When the dust from two whirlwind days of qualifying had settled, Foyt had put himself into the show. "Welcome to Foyt's house," proclaimed a sign in the Indianapolis Motor Speedway stands on race day. He thrilled the crowd of more than 300,000 by briefly shooting as high as second place. Mechanical troubles soon dashed his chances, but Foyt had shown, a few months shy of his sixtieth birthday, that he could still hang in there with the best of them.

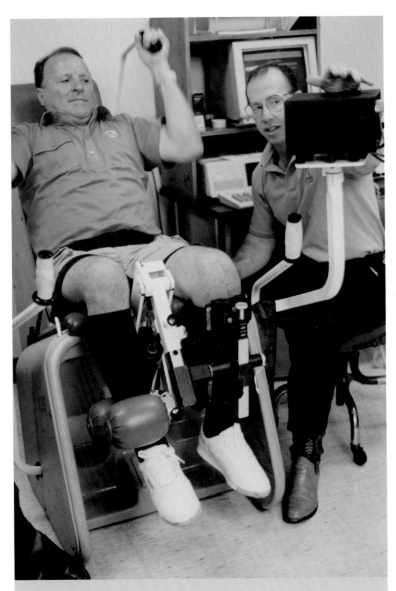

Houston Oilers' trainer Steve Watterson (right) helps Foyt with his rehabilitation after Foyt broke both of his legs in a crash.

After Foyt retired from driving, he continued to participate in motor sports as the owner of Foyt Racing. As both driver and team owner, Foyt had already won national Indycar titles in 1967, 1975, and 1979. Now that he was out of the cockpit, he focused his competitive drive on succeeding as a team owner. It didn't take him long to produce a winner. In 1996, Foyt Racing's Scott Sharp was the cochampion of the Indy Racing League (**IRL**) series. Foyt Racing's Kenny Brack won the IRL championship in 1998 and finished second the following year. The highlight of

A.J. Foyt stands next to his #50 Copenhagen Ford and waves to the crowd prior to the 1994 Brickyard 400. Foyt could not resist participating in the first stock car race held at the Indianapolis Speedway.

Foyt Racing's 1998 championship season occurred when Brack captured the checkered flag at the Indianapolis 500. It was the first time Foyt had been in the winner's circle at Indy when he was not himself the driver of the winning car. Foyt Racing continued having successes, but the team garnered no championships to show for its efforts.

In 2005, Foyt hoped for his sixth win at the Indy 500. His team placed three cars in the race's starting grid. Foyt's son Larry and Brazilian driver Felipe Giaffone piloted two of the cars. Most of the attention, however, was focused on the third driver: A.J.'s grandson, Anthony Foyt IV. Two years earlier, at age 19, he had been the youngest driver ever

A.J. Foyt IV *(left)* and Larry Foyt carry on the family racing tradition.

to qualify at the Indy 500 and had finished in eighteenth place. As the race started, Larry Foyt began experiencing trouble with his car. Despite making a pit stop to change tires, the car continued to drive poorly. On lap 15, Larry's car lost power and spun out, slamming into the wall on turn 2. Larry was taken to the hospital, where he was diagnosed with a back injury and released the next day. Things did not go well for Anthony Foyt, either. On lap 77, his car bumped a passing car in a turn. Anthony was able to coax his hobbled racer back into the pit, but the damage was too great for him to continue. Giaffone, who started in last place, drove his car well and finished in the fifteenth slot. Despite the disappointments, A.J. Foyt was proud. It was the forty-eighth straight year that he had participated in the Indianapolis 500 as an owner, a driver, or both. The three Foyt Racing cars sported stickers celebrating this achievement.

Foyt now lives with his wife, Lucy, in Houston, Texas. In addition to Foyt Racing, he owns cattle and horse ranches and the largest auto dealership in Texas. He also has business interests in oil wells, a hotel chain, and the largest funeral service business in the country.

Foyt's daughter, Terry, works as a real estate agent. All three of his sons—Tony III, Jerry, and Larry—are involved in motor sports. A.J. Foyt discouraged his sons from becoming drivers, but one—Larry—could not resist. Larry is actually A.J. Foyt's grandson, but his grandparents adopted him after his parents divorced. Larry considers A.J. and Lucy his parents. After graduating from Texas Christian University, Larry spent several years learning the racing ropes. He raced his own car in NASCAR's minor league, the Busch Series. In 2003, he made his debut in

NASCAR's major league, the Winston Cup Series, driving for his father's NASCAR team. The following year, he drove in his first Indianapolis 500. An accident in lap 54 forced him out of the race. Larry's bad luck at Indy continued in 2005. He crashed in lap 14, injuring his back, and ended up missing the rest of the racing season. Larry returned for the 2006 Indy 500, but car trouble forced him out after only 43 laps.

The legendary A.J. Foyt lives in Houston, Texas, and is the owner of Foyt Racing.

Anthony Foyt, Tony III's son, also decided to enter his grandfather's profession. He started racing junior dragsters at age 13 and moved up to go-karts the next year. In 2002, Anthony won the IRL Infiniti Pro Series season championship. The following year, he moved up to the IRL's big leagues, the IndyCar Series. On his 19th birthday, Anthony became the youngest driver ever to compete in the Indianapolis 500. He continued to drive for his grandfather's IndyCar team but had poor finishes in many races, including the 2004 and 2005 Indy 500. After the 2005 season, the Akins Motorsports team hired Anthony to drive one of its cars in NASCAR's Busch Series. A change in ownership at Akins, however, resulted in the young driver's being dropped from the team before the start of the 2006 season. In September 2006, the Andretti Green racing team asked Anthony to step in to replace an injured driver. He finished in fourteenth place in the Peak Antifreeze Indy 300, the last race of the 2006 IndyCar Series season. The youngest Foyt is certain to carry on the family's racing legacy. He has asserted, "I plan on racing the rest of my life, no matter what kind of cars."

Now in his seventies, A.J. Foyt continues to participate in racing, enjoying as an owner the thrills that he experienced during his illustrious career as a driver. Foyt Racing has found little success over the years, but its owner keeps on going. Larry Foyt has observed about his father, "If there's one thing he's not, it's a quitter." A.J. Foyt once summed up his approach to racing and life: "I could never settle for being anything but the best. I've always loved racing more than anything in my life and if I couldn't be the best at it, my life wouldn't mean much to me."

# STATISTICS

## Indianapolis 500

Total Starts: 35

| Year | Starting Position | Average Speed (in mph) |
|---|---|---|
| **Wins** | | |
| 1961 | 7 | 139.130 |
| 1964 | 5 | 147.350 |
| 1967 | 4 | 151.207 |
| 1977 | 4 | 161.331 |

**Pole Positions**

| Year | Qualifying Speed (in mph) |
|---|---|
| 1965 | 161.233 |
| 1969 | 170.568 |
| 1974 | 191.632 |
| 1975 | 193.976 |

**Career Statistics**

IndyCar Wins: 67
IndyCar Pole Positions: 53
NASCAR Wins: 8
Sports Car Wins: 5
USAC National Championships: 7 (1960, 1961, 1963, 1964, 1967, 1975, 1979)
USAC Midget Car Wins: 22
USAC Sprint Car Wins: 27
USAC Stock Car Wins: 44
Total Major Events Won: 173

# CHRONOLOGY

**1935** Anthony Joseph Foyt Jr. is born in Houston, Texas, on January 16.

**1953** A.J. Foyt begins professional racing career at Houston area tracks.

**1955** Marries Lucy Zarr; begins racing sprint cars.

**1956** Son, Anthony Joseph III, is born.

**1957** Wins first USAC race, in Kansas City, Missouri.

**1958** Races in the Indianapolis 500; daughter, Terry, is born.

**1960** Wins USAC National Championship.

**1961** Wins Indianapolis 500; wins USAC National Championship.

**1962** Son, Jerry, is born.

**1963** Wins USAC National Championship.

**1964** Wins Indianapolis 500; wins Daytona Firecracker 400; breaks record for most career Indy Car wins; wins USAC National Championship.

**1966** End of Foyt's record streak of 82 consecutive Indy Car starts.

**1967** Hires father, Tony Foyt, as head mechanic; wins Indianapolis 500; with Dan Gurney wins the 24 Hours of Le Mans; wins USAC National Championship.

**1972** Wins Daytona 500.

**1975** Wins USAC National Championship.

**1977** Wins fourth and final Indianapolis 500.

**1979** Wins USAC National Championship; adopts grandson Larry.

**1985** Wins 12 Hours of Sebring sports car race.

**1991** Qualifies for first row at Indianapolis 500.

1992  Races in thirty-fifth consecutive Indianapolis 500.

1993  Announces retirement at Indianapolis Motor Speedway.

1994  Races in inaugural Brickyard 400 stock car race.

1998  Leads Foyt Racing to IRL Championship with driver Kenny Brack; Brack wins Indianapolis 500.

2005  Watches three Foyt Racing drivers, including Larry Foyt and A.J. Foyt IV, compete in the Indianapolis 500.

2006  Involved in the Indianapolis 500 for forty-ninth consecutive year as driver or owner.

2007  Foyt celebrates his 50th year in IndyCar racing.

# GLOSSARY

**checkered flag**—The flag (with a checkerboard design) that is waved when the winner of a race crosses the finish line.

**IRL**—Indy Racing League, an organization that oversees races in the United States involving open-wheel cars (race cars with wheels mounted outside the main body).

**lap**—One complete circuit around a racetrack.

**NASCAR**—The National Association for Stock Car Auto Racing, the organization that oversees both stock car and other types of races.

**pole position**—The number-one starting position, usually earned by having the fastest car during qualifying.

**qualifying run**—A system of timed trials held before races, used to establish which drivers are eligible for the race and to determine the drivers' positions on the starting grid.

**stock car**—Race cars that have similar bodies to automobiles sold to the general public; NASCAR racing cars.

**turbo/turbine**—A motor system that injects a greater amount of air into the engine's cylinders, producing more power than in conventional engines.

**USAC**—The United States Automobile Club, the organization that formerly oversaw open-wheel (Indy car) racing.

**yellow flag**—The flag that is waved when there is a hazard on the racetrack, such as an accident, debris, or a wet surface; drivers must slow down and cannot pass another car.

# BIBLIOGRAPHY

Engel, Lyle Kenyon. *The Incredible A.J. Foyt*. New York: Arco Publishing Co., 1970.

Foyt, A.J., with William Neely. *A.J.* New York: Times Books, 1983.

Golenbock, Peter. *American Zoom*. New York: Macmillan, 1993.

Higdon, Hal. *Finding the Groove*. New York: G.P. Putnam's Sons, 1973.

Jezierski, Chet. *Speed! IndyCar Racing*. New York: Harry N. Abrams, 1985.

Johnson, Alan. *Driving in Competition*. New York: W.W. Norton and Co., 1971.

Kleinfield, Sonny. *A Month at the Brickyard*. New York: Holt, Rinehart and Winston, 1977.

Libby, Bill. *Andretti*. New York: Grosset & Dunlap, 1970.

Libby, Bill. *Foyt*. New York: Hawthorn Books, Inc., 1974.

Libby, Bill, and Richard Petty. *King Richard: The Richard Petty Story*. New York: Doubleday, 1977.

Moran, Malcolm. "Defying the Odds at Indy." *The New York Times Magazine*, May 25, 1986, 32.

Nack, William. "Twilight of a Titan." *Sports Illustrated*, September 30, 1991, 67.

Ottum, Bob. "Get Out of the Way, Here Comes A.J." *Sports Illustrated*, May 25, 1981, 99.

Scalzo, Joe, and Bobby Unser. *The Bobby Unser Story*. New York: Doubleday, 1979.

Stewart, Mark. *Auto Racing: A History of Fast Cars and Fearless Drivers*. Danbury, Conn.: Franklin Watts, 1998.

Yates, Brock, W. *Sunday Driver*. New York: Fireside, 1990.

# FURTHER READING

Arute, Jack, with Jenna Fryer. *Jack Arute's Tales from the Indy 500*, with a foreword by A.J. Foyt. Champaign, Ill.: Sports Publishing, 2006.

Engel, Lyle Kenyon. *The Incredible A.J. Foyt*. New York: Arco Publishing Co., 1970.

Foyt, A.J., with William Neely. *A.J.* New York: Times Books, 1983.

Fish, Bruce, and Becky Durost Fish. *Indy Car Racing*. Langhorne, Pa.: Chelsea House, 2001.

Gillispie, Tom, ed. *Racing Families: A Tribute to Racing's Fastest Dynasties*. Dallas: Beckett, 2000.

Golenbock, Peter, and Greg Fielden, eds. *NASCAR Encyclopedia*. St. Paul, Minn.: Motorbooks International, 2003.

Libby, Bill. *Foyt*. New York: Hawthorn Books, Inc., 1974.

Martin, James A., and Thomas F. Saal. *American Auto Racing: The Milestones and Personalities of a Century of Speed*. Jefferson, N.C.: McFarland & Co., 2004.

Prentzas, G.S. *Mario Andretti*. New York: Chelsea House, 2007.

## WEB SITES

www.foytracing.com
The official site for Foyt Racing includes information about A.J. Foyt, Larry Foyt, and A.J. Foyt IV.

www.brickyard.com
This site offers the history of and a schedule for the Indianapolis Motor Speedway.

www.indycar.com
The official site for the Indy Racing League provides video clips, driver biographies, fan club information, and more.

www.mshf.com
The Motorsports Hall of Fame site provides information about the Motorsports Museum as well as media downloads.

# PICTURE CREDITS

**page:**

8:   Courtesy of the Foyt Family
10:  Courtesy of the Foyt Family
14:  Courtesy of the Foyt Family
15:  Courtesy of the Foyt Family
17:  Courtesy of the Foyt Family
18:  Courtesy of the Foyt Family
21:  © Artemis Images
22:  IMS Photo
23:  IMS Photo
25:  Courtesy of the Foyt Family
28:  IMS Photo
29:  IMS Photo
32:  IMS Photo
34:  © AP Images
35:  IMS Photo

37:  © Bettmann/CORBIS
40:  IMS Photo
41:  IMS Photo
42:  © Bettmann/CORBIS
43:  IMS Photo
45:  IMS Photo
46:  © Bettmann/CORBIS
48:  © AFP/Getty Images
49:  © Bettmann/CORBIS
51:  IMS Photo
53:  © Bettmann/CORBIS
55:  © Bettmann/CORBIS
57:  Courtesy of Anne Fornoro
58:  IMS Photo
59:  IMS Photo
61:  IMS Photo

**Cover:**
A.J. Foyt climbs out of his Chevrolet after claiming the pole position with the field's fastest lap in preparation for the Firecracker 400, which was held on July 4, 1976, at Daytona International Speedway in Daytona Beach. (© MTF/AP Images)

# INDEX

# ABOUT THE AUTHORS

**JOSH WILKER** has a degree in writing and literature from Johnson State College. He is the author of numerous children's biographies and history books, including a biography of Julius Erving for Chelsea House.

**G.S. PRENTZAS** is an editor and writer who lives in New York. He has written a dozen books for young readers, including a guide to the 1994 Winter Olympics and a biography of football great Jim Brown. He is also the author of *Mario Andretti* in Chelsea House's series RACE CAR LEGENDS: COLLECTOR'S EDITION.